globe-trotters CLUB

Mexico

Tom Streissguth

❧ Carolrhoda Books, Inc. / Minneapolis

Photo Acknowledgments

Photos, maps, and artworks are used courtesy of: Laura Westlund, pp. 1, 2-3, 4, 7, 9, 20, 26-27, 35, 37, 41; © Nik Wheeler, pp. 5 (top), 10, 12, 13 (left and right), 16 (top), 18, 22, 26, 28, 30, 32, 34, 35, 38, 39 (left), 41, 42; © Mike Reed, pp. 5 (bottom), 23 (right), 45; David Mangurian, p. 6; © Chuck Place, pp. 6-7, 25, 27, 44; © Buddy Mays/TRAVEL STOCK, pp. 8, 9, 14 (left and middle), 15, 16 (bottom); John Erste, pp. 11, 13, 22, 24, 28, 32; Paula Jansen, pp. 14 (right), 19, 20, 21, 33; Museum of Modern Art of Latin America, p. 17 (top); Phillips Bourns, p. 17 (bottom); © Monica V. Brown, pp. 18 (inset), 23 (left), 37; Tom Moran, pp. 24, 31, 40; Robert L. and Diane Wolfe, pp. 29, 43; Independent Picture Service, p. 36; Schalkwijk/Art Resource, NY, p. 39 (right). Cover photo of pottery masks © Nik Wheeler.

Carolrhoda Books, Inc.
c/o The Lerner Publishing Group
241 First Avenue North
Minneapolis, Minnesota 55401 U.S.A.

Words in **bold type** are explained in a glossary that begins on page 44.

Library of Congress Cataloging-in-Publication Data

Streissguth, Thomas, 1958-
    Mexico / by Tom Streissguth.
        p.   cm. — (Globe-trotters club)
    Includes index.
    Summary: Examines the geography, society, and culture of Mexico.
    ISBN 1-57505-100-1 (lib. bdg. : alk. paper)
    1. Mexico-Juvenile literature. [1. Mexico.] I. Title.
II. Series: Globe-trotters club (Series)
F1208.5.S77   1997
917.2—dc 21   95-51781

Contents

¡Bienvenidos a **México!***

*That's "Welcome to Mexico" in Spanish, the official language of Mexico.

Where in the world can you cross a river and travel from one United States to another? At the Rio Grande. This long river winds its way between the United States of America and the Estados Unidos Mexicanos. In Spanish the name means United Mexican States. It's the official name of Mexico. The country is made up of 31 states and a federal district—Mexico City.

On a map, Mexico looks like a long, curving funnel. Mexico's border with the United States sits at the top of the funnel, at the Rio Grande, a waterway that Mexicans call the Río Bravo del Norte.

The nations of Guatemala and Belize are Mexico's southern neighbors. Along this border, **tropical rain forests** (dense forests with heavy rainfall) cover steep mountainsides. The weather report here is always the same—humid and warm, with an occasional **hurricane,** or strong ocean storm.

Mexico's tropical rain forests (left) lie in the southeast. The Río Bravo del Norte, or the Great Northern River, (below) separates Mexico from the United States.

ϾϾϾ	mountains
∴∴∴	deserts
═══	plains
⋎⋎⋎	rain forests
⌇⌇⌇	valleys
▲	volcanoes
▪	historical sites
────	state borders

Coast to **Coast**

No matter where you are in Mexico, you're never more than about 900 miles from a sea. That's because Mexico is almost entirely surrounded by water. The Pacific Ocean meets the country's long western coast. Here a narrow **peninsula**—land surrounded on three sides by water—stretches into the Pacific. This finger of land is Baja California. Large black-and-orange Gila monsters and other poisonous lizards scramble among the rocks and cacti. But not many people live in Baja's dry, hot **deserts.**

On the eastern side of Mexico is the Gulf of Mexico. Shrimping boats sail into the Gulf from the busy port of Veracruz. Tall oil rigs rise offshore, pumping crude oil from beneath the seafloor.

Yucatán, another peninsula, reaches into the Gulf. See if you can locate Yucatán on the map on page four. This peninsula is unlike the rest of Mexico. It's as flat as a pancake. In some places, small houses built of palm leaves appear alongside the roads. Maya Indians make their homes in Yucatán.

Hundreds of ancient cities are hidden in the forests of Yucatán. Some haven't even been found yet. People would have to cut new paths through the trees to reach these hidden cities, which the Maya built many, many years ago.

Mexicans of all ages (left) **enjoy dodging waves on the country's sandy beaches. Crews will soon take these boats** (below) **from the port of Campeche into the waters of the Gulf of Mexico to catch fish.**

Fast Facts about Mexico

Name: Estados Unidos Mexicanos (United Mexican States)

Area: 756,066 square miles

Main Landforms: Western Sierra Madre, Eastern Sierra Madre, Southern Sierra Madre, Baja California, Yucatán Peninsula, Meseta Central

Highest Point: Orizaba (18,698 feet)

Lowest Point: Sea level

Animals: Gila monsters, monarch butterflies, flamingoes, ocelots, spider monkeys, coatamundis, gray whales

Capital City: Mexico City

Other Major Cities: Monterrey, Guadalajara, Puebla, Veracruz, Ciudad Juárez

Official Language: Spanish

Monetary Unit: Peso

Getting
Around

The cars of this train curve along a track that goes from Los Mochis near the Gulf of California through the Copper Canyon to Chihuahua.

 There are fast ways and slow ways to travel in Mexico. Cars share the roads with trucks, buses, and sometimes even horses and burros (donkeys). Trains chug across the plains and through the valleys. Some farmers haul their crops to market on horse-drawn carts, while airplanes criss-cross the skies above. If you were in Mexico, what sort of ride would you choose?

Careful! Going from place to place in Mexico can be dangerous. Steep mountains cover most of the country. Two long ranges run north to south, like side-by-side railroad tracks. The Eastern Sierra Madre is in the east, and the Western Sierra Madre rises in the west. The Sierra Madres separate the coasts from a high **plateau,** or level plain, in the center of the country.

The plateau is called the Meseta Central. Here many people work as ranchers or miners. The dry climate of the plateau makes it a nice place to live. Most of Mexico's large cities lie on the Meseta.

In the cities, people crowd the sidewalks and plazas (town squares). Many city dwellers don't own cars. They walk to work, to shops, or to church. If it's too far to walk, they'll take a bus. Some people use bikes or motor scooters to get around.

Getting around in Mexico City, the overcrowded capital (government center), is a challenge. The city sprawls in every direction.

¡Hola!
Today we took a great train ride through the Copper Canyon, which is as big as the Grand Canyon in the United States. In Spanish the Copper Canyon is called Barranca del Cobre. We started at Chihuahua (the city, not the dog!) and ended at Los Mochis, a town on the west coast. The train crossed 39 bridges and went through 85 tunnels! (I counted!) Mountains and cliffs towered on both sides of the tracks. Several times a steep, scary drop-off appeared right next to the train. I closed my eyes when that happened. Tomorrow we're taking a boat to Baja California. Wish you were here!
¡Adios, Amigos!

Farmers in the Mexican countryside often use carts to get around. How tall do you think this farmer's stack of corn husks is?

Cars, taxis, buses, and trucks jam the roads. Travelers can go beneath the streets to take the subway, an underground train. Or they can flag down a *colectivo*—a van that hauls passengers on a fixed route through the city.

In the countryside, far from any town or village, people walk on the sides of roads. Where are they going? They may be heading to work in the fields. They may be carrying holiday gifts to relatives. Or they may be going to a marketplace to sell their goods.

Down in
the Valley

 Mexico City was built on the floor of a large **basin** of land called the Valley of Mexico. From the air, this region looks like a huge salad bowl, with mountains making up the sides of the bowl. Hundreds of years ago, shallow lakes and **marshes** covered the valley. These days it's the site of the biggest city in the world. Sometimes Mexico City is called a **megalopolis,** which means a very large city. People complain about the capital's air pollution, which is some of the world's worst. That's because the surrounding mountains hold in the city's smoke and dust.

In this same spot, Aztec Indians once lived in a city called Tenochtitlán. They built canals, bridges, and causeways (raised roads constructed over water). Huge temples shaped

Mountains ring Mexico City, the biggest city not only in Mexico but in the entire world! Sometimes, though, it's hard to see the mountains because of the thick smog. Children are told to stay inside when the air pollution is really bad. For a few coins, streetside machines offer strollers a sip of clean, fresh oxygen, and laws ban certain cars from the downtown area every day.

like pyramids rose from the valley floor.

In the 1500s, explorers from Spain conquered the Aztecs. Spain is a country in Europe—a long way from Mexico! The Europeans filled in the lakes and tore down the pyramids. They built new homes and churches in their own style. In the Spanish language, the new colony was known as Nueva España (New Spain).

The Aztec site of Tenochtitlán became Mexico City, the capital city of Nueva España. The city grew around a central square called the Zócalo. The Zócalo is huge. It's the second-largest square in the entire world. Only Red Square in Moscow, Russia, is bigger.

Old and new buildings sit side by side in Mexico City. Some of the older buildings look a little unsteady, as if they are losing their balance. They're leaning because their foundations are shifting in the soft, swampy soil.

According to legend, the Aztecs built Tenochtitlán on the spot where an eagle was seen perched on a cactus eating a snake. But eagles no longer fly over the Valley of Mexico. Brown smoke from cars and factories fills the air. The pollution stings your eyes and makes it hard to breathe. The only eagle you'll see in Mexico City is the one on the Mexican flag.

Twin **Peaks**

Giant twin **volcanoes** rise south of Mexico City. One is named Popocatépetl, which means "smoking mountain" in the Aztec language. At times, "Popo" lets off a little smoke. The other volcano, called Iztaccíhuatl, is inactive.

Farther south tower the Southern Sierra Madre. Near this mountain range is a tropical rain forest, where spider monkeys, ocelots, and jaguars live. Mangoes, bananas, papayas, and other kinds of tasty fruit thrive in the wet, steamy climate.

What's a spider monkey? A spider monkey uses its tail to hang from trees. When it's dangling from a limb, a spider monkey looks like a gigantic spider. Yikes!

The forest is also home to many small villages of native peoples, who haven't changed their way of life for thousands of years. Some of these Indians use their own languages instead of Spanish.

(Facing page) **A church sits in the shadow of snowcapped Popocatépetl.** (Above left) **Southeast of the peak are tropical rain forests that hold sweet mangoes and other fruits.** (Above) **The forests of Yucatán supply local native peoples with wood and other materials.**

(Left) **A cornseller from the south**

Mexico is home to people from many different ethnic backgrounds, including a **farmboy** (above) from the Baja region of the northwest.

(Above) **A pair of rollerbladers from Guaymas**

Who's a **Mexican?**

People of many different backgrounds live in Mexico. But, at one time, *indígenas* (native peoples) were the only ones there. Before the Europeans arrived, Olmecs, Aztecs, Toltecs, Maya, and hundreds of other groups lived in the countryside at different periods.

Then came the Spanish **Conquest,** or takeover, of Mexico in the 1500s. Mexicans call it La Conquista. Everybody in Mexico knows about La Conquista. It was a major turning point in Mexican history. Mexico became a **colony** of Spain. Many Spanish colonists came to live in Mexico and married Indians. The children of these mixed marriages are called mestizos.

Most of the 93.7 million people in Mexico are mestizos. About 8 million Mexicans are indígenas—from more than 50 different Indian groups. Two smaller **ethnic groups** join the mix. Criollos are people with only Spanish or European ancestors. Some criollos come from the United States or Canada. The ancestors of mulattoes were Africans brought to Mexico as slaves. They married mestizos, Indians, or criollos.

What's in a Name?

- Mexico comes from Mexica, the name the Aztecs used for themselves.
- Mexicans call their neighbors to the north of the Río Bravo *norteamericanos*.

15

First **Peoples**

Stone pyramids at Uxmal, Chichén Itzá, Palenque, and other places are reminders of Mexico's early peoples, such as the Aztec and the Maya. Foreign tourists as well as Mexicans visit these ancient sites every year.

Some parts of Mexico still have large indígena populations. The Maya live in the southern states of Chiapas and Yucatán. Oaxaca is the home of the Mixtec and the Zapotec. A very popular Mexican president named Benito Juarez was a Zapotec Indian.

Few Spanish settlers wanted to live in southern Mexico. The land is forested, mountainous, and not good for growing crops. This region is the poorest in the country and not many roads exist. In some places, there are no schools or hospitals.

José Clemente Orozco painted this image of Benito Juárez (1806–1872), who is sometimes called the Abraham Lincoln of Mexico. Juárez served as president of Mexico at about the same time Lincoln was U.S. president. Both came from humble backgrounds—and both even wore tall hats!

Small groups of nomads live in northern Mexico, where it's dry and hot. These are the Seri, who are called nomads because they move from one place to another in search of food, water, and firewood.

Some of Mexico's Indians speak little Spanish. They use their own languages to talk to one another. They speak Spanish only when necessary. In Yucatán, for example, you may hear people using Mayan as well as Spanish.

This Mayan girl can trace her heritage to among Mexico's earliest and most advanced cultures.

17

¡Que **Problema!**

Mexico has a problem. Its population is growing very, very fast. Many Mexicans live in overcrowded cities. One out of every five citizens—or 19 million people—lives in Mexico City. An enormous amount of water and food must be brought into the city every day. Meanwhile, thousands of people from the countryside move to this gigantic megalopolis daily. (There's that crazy word again!)

Most of these people are looking for work. But many can't afford a house or an apartment. So they move to the outskirts of the city and build small houses of tin or plywood. Neighborhoods like these usually

Newcomers to the crowded capital often don't have jobs so they can't afford proper housing. Just to get by, these people build flimsy shelters (inset) **that don't have plumbing. This is a big problem in places like Mexico City.**

don't have clean water or indoor plumbing. Sicknesses can spread easily in such places.

Traffic and people crowd the cities of Mexico. Groups of abandoned children live on the sidewalks. Some of them are **orphans** and others just have no place to stay. These children don't have a home and they don't go to school.

To find a better life, some Mexicans seek jobs in the United States. After they arrive, many of these **immigrants** (people who move into another country) work in factories, on farms, or in people's homes. They often make less money than other workers in the United States. But they may earn much more than they could in Mexico. Many send money home to their families.

Some immigrants cross the border in secret because they don't have permission to live in the neighboring country. They are taking a risk to live and work in the United States. If the U.S. Border Patrol catches them, they are sent back to Mexico.

Although many people in Mexico live with hardship, not everyone in Mexico is poor. Some families live in nice houses, the parents have good jobs, and the children have plenty to eat.

Family *Values*

Mexican households can be very large. Many couples have three, four, or more children. Families sometimes share their home with relatives—aunts, uncles, cousins, and grandparents.

Quinceañera

When a Mexican girl turns 15, her family throws a big party called a *quinceañera*. The birthday marks her passing from girlhood to womanhood. Girls look forward to their quinceañeras, because they are allowed to stay up later in the evenings and sometimes get their own bedrooms.

An extended family—one that includes older and younger relatives—enjoys a day at the beach.

All in the Family

Here are the Spanish words for family members. Practice using these terms on your own family. See if they can understand you!

father	*padre*	(PAH-dray)
mother	*madre*	(MAH-dray)
uncle	*tío*	(TEE-oh)
aunt	*tía*	(TEE-ah)
grandfather	*abuelo*	(ah-BWAY-loh)
grandmother	*abuela*	(ah-BWAY-lah)
son	*hijo*	(EE-hoh)
daughter	*hija*	(EE-hah)
brother	*hermano*	(ehr-MAH-noh)
sister	*hermana*	(ehr-MAH-nah)

Grandparents help with household chores and with raising children. The older folks freely give advice. The younger generation respects its elders. Grown-up sons and daughters feel a responsibility to take care of their aging family members.

In towns and cities, housing often sits very close to the street. Balconies, such as these on a street in Puebla, give residents more space.

In the **Neighborhood**

The streets in Mexican cities are lively. ¡Hola! People greet their friends on the sidewalks. Honk! Cars, buses, and motor scooters speed by on the road. ¡He! At the street market, people shout, haggle, laugh, and praise the wares.

Rows of stone houses sit right next to the narrow sidewalk. If two people must pass, one of them may have to give up the sidewalk and step out into the street. It's the polite thing to do. Brightly painted houses sport iron grilles on their windows. Passing through the front door reveals a quiet patio. On the second story, a long balcony surrounds the courtyard. Doors and windows face the patio. The doors lead to rooms or private apartments. The Spanish colonists built this kind of house in Mexico to look like the houses they knew in Spain. Not all families have colonial-style houses.

22

called azoteas. A student who can't afford a regular apartment may live in an azotea.

Many city dwellers live in high-rise apartments. Others make their homes on the outskirts of towns. The Mexican government built homes here to replace unhealthy **shanty-towns,** or slums. Mexicans call these new developments *colonías,* which means colonies.

In the Mexican countryside, small houses are usually made of adobe. This is clay that is mixed, formed into bricks, and then dried in the sun. The roofs are made of red clay tiles. Mexico's Indians may live in other kinds of houses. In Yucatán the Maya build small dwellings out of branches, reeds, and thatch. They sleep in hammocks hung above the ground or on straw mats on the floor.

Mexicans build houses out of everything from bricks that have been painted in pastel colors (left) **to young trees and palm leaves** (above).

23

Mexican
Munchies

In some ways, Mexican food hasn't changed in thousands of years. The ancient Indians raised corn and beans, which are still common in Mexico. The early Mexicans also ate papayas, bananas, potatoes, and avocadoes. Before the Conquest, no European had ever tasted these foods!

Salsa

Salsa (fresh tomato sauce) is a tasty addition to almost any Mexican dish. Ask a grownup to help you make your very own. This recipe yields about three cups.

You will need:
6 medium-sized tomatoes, chopped
½ cup chopped canned green chilies
⅓ cup chopped onion
I teaspoon salt

Combine the finely chopped vegetables listed above in a bowl. Add as much of the salt as tastes good to you.

(Facing page) **Twirling a *molinillo*, or wooden stirring tool, a girl makes creamy hot chocolate, a favorite breakfast drink in Mexico.** (Above) **Corn, when ground into flour, is an ingredient of tortillas, but the husk can also be filled to make a tamale.**

For breakfast many Mexicans have hot chocolate and a sweet roll. They may also eat a plate of eggs with beans that are boiled, mashed, and fried. In some homes, lunch is the main meal of the day. But other families—especially those in cities—have a big evening meal instead.

One of the most popular Mexican foods is the tortilla, a thin, flat cornmeal pancake. Several are served with every meal, just like bread. Tortillas can be fixed in many different ways. Filling a tortilla with meat and cheese makes a taco. Bake a tortilla, after filling it with stuffing and covering it with sauce, and it's an enchilada.

Tortillas are also fast food. Small tortilla shops can be found almost everywhere in Mexico. Other stands sell tamales—steamed husks of corn filled with combinations of cornmeal, meat, beans, fish, and spices. By peeling back the husks, you can eat the stuffings inside.

Thanks to a little fellow called the chile pepper, Mexican food is often spicy. More than 100 different kinds of chiles are grown. Jalapeños are firecracker hot, other chiles are milder. If the chiles are too hot, people grab a fruit drink. But lots of Mexicans prefer orange soda or cola instead.

Where would you go to buy everything you need? The answer is the *mercado*, or Mexican market, where stalls selling fruits, vegetables, meat, candy, jewelry, and clothing jostle for space.

A Trip to
the Market

Many Mexican homes have tiny refrigerators. Others have no refrigerators at all. Food won't stay fresh for long at room temperature, which can be quite warm in Mexico. That's why it's common for Mexicans to shop regularly at an outdoor market called a *mercado*.

The mercado opens very early and often runs all day long. In large cities, the mercado fills a huge building that's partially open to the street. Merchant stalls line the sides and aisles of the space. Shoppers can buy food, clothing, household items, jewelry, and other goods there. In small towns, farmers from the countryside sell their crops. They weigh the fruits and vegetables on a scale for customers. They may also have chickens, birds, ducklings, or turkeys for sale. Iguana sellers offer the colorful lizards as pets.

Some people visit the market just to eat at small food stands or cafes.

Taco stands are popular fast-food stops at the markets.

Pots and pans rattle on a stove behind a counter. Customers stroll along the street, visiting the stands, looking for a good dish. They settle down at a counter to enjoy steamed tamales, tacos, or enchiladas.

The market bustles with people on foot, with motor scooters, with delivery wagons, and with bicycles. Vendors greet friends and familiar customers and exchange the latest news. The mercado is the crossroads of the community!

In Mexico some people chain their pet iguanas to keep them from running away— much the way you would tie up a dog. Can you imagine a lizard on a leash?

Let's **Fiesta!**

In Mexico a special party is called a fiesta. At least once a year—sometimes more often—every town and village in Mexico has a big fiesta. Fiestas are held on national and religious holidays. Some fiestas mark special days on the Christian calendar, such as

During fiestas, young Mexicans dress in colorful clothing, participate in parades, listen to music, and enjoy fireworks. These girls are part of Cinco de Mayo, a holiday that celebrates May 5, 1862, when Mexican forces defeated the French army at the Battle of Puebla.

Important Mexican Holidays

How do the holidays listed below compare to the ones you and your family celebrate?

January 1	New Year's Day
February 5	Constitution Day (marks signing in 1914 of Mexican constitution)
March 21	Birthday of Benito Juárez
May 5	Cinco de Mayo (marks Mexican victory over French at Battle of Puebla, 1862)
May 10	Mother's Day
September 16	Independence Day
October 12	Day of the Race (Columbus Day)
November 2	Day of the Dead
November 20	Anniversary of the Mexican Revolution
December 12	Feast of the Virgin of Guadalupe
December 25	Christmas

Semana Santa (Holy Week, the week before Easter). Others celebrate a saint's day.

During the fiesta, school is out and work stops. Everyone in town gathers at the plaza for a fun time. Bands play in the corners of the square. People greet their friends, laugh, and sing. Piñatas—colorfully decorated containers filled with candy and small toys—are hung from trees or ceilings. Blindfolded children try to bust open the piñatas with a wooden stick. People shout and fireworks go off. Spinning fireworks explode on a *torito*, a frame shaped like a bull. Some cities have mock bullfights. Cars honk and motor scooters dash through the streets. The celebration runs into the early morning hours, with colorful lights decorating the neighborhoods. It may even go on for another day or two! Nobody gets much sleep during a fiesta.

Day of the Dead

Mexicans celebrate a unique festival called Día de los Muertos, or Day of the Dead, on November 2 each year. This holiday may remind you of Halloween, because sometimes people dress up in costumes. But in fact, it's a time to remember family members who have died. Families create *offrendas*—offerings of food and flowers—to honor these relatives. They eat special candies shaped like skulls or coffins! In the evenings, they picnic near their relative's graves, which they have decorated with marigold flowers. But Día de los Muertos isn't really scary or sad. It's meant to be a celebration!

School
Days

At most schools in Mexico—whether state-run or private— uniforms are part of the gear for boys and girls. Students take subjects, such as math and reading, that will help them find a good job.

Life in Mexico is not all fun and games. Beginning at the age of six, Mexican children go to school. They have six years of elementary school, then three years of middle school. Students study math, geography, reading, biology, and history.

After middle school, some students start working. Others go to high school and then on to college. Many Mexican schools have modern equipment, such as computers. But other schools, especially in poor rural areas, have very little besides a room and desks. There may not be enough books to go around. The classrooms may be crowded. In these areas, some children work at home or on their family's farm. They don't go to school, or they go for just a few years.

About eight out of every ten Mexicans can read and write. In some cities, signs and symbols help those who cannot read. In Mexico City, for example, signs in subway stations carry words as well as pictures.

Meet Paula María

Paula María Fosada is 10 years old and goes to a public school in southern Mexico. Each morning her mother walks her to school, where Paula María studies from 8:00 A.M. to 1:00 P.M. In the afternoon, Paula María completes her homework and a few chores before she is allowed to play. Does Paula María's schedule sound familiar?

Most Mexicans belong to the Roman Catholic religion. Fiestas mark Roman Catholic holidays, such as Good Friday and Easter. Catholics may begin the fiesta by going to church. Afterward, they may walk in a parade holding pictures of Jesus, the Virgin Mary, or their city's patron saint.

Faith and
Fiestas

Most people in Mexico belong to the Roman Catholic Church. This was the church of the Spanish conquerors and settlers. After the Conquest, **missionaries** came from Spain to teach the indígenas about the religion. Some Indians accepted the Catholic faith.

Many also held on to their own religious traditions.

Although they tried, the Spaniards did not get rid of Indian religions. The Tarahumara people, who live near Copper Canyon, still worship the spirits of the sun, the moon, and the rain. The Maya and the Zapotec continue to practice old rituals and beliefs.

Over the years, Catholic and native ideas have mixed in many ways. Catholics in Mexico celebrate their holidays with long fiestas. During a fiesta, you may see people wearing Aztec costumes and headdresses. They perform dances that existed long before Catholicism arrived.

December 12

On December 12, Catholics from all over the country visit a Mexico City shrine— where a saint is honored—to worship the Virgin of Guadalupe. The shrine marks the spot where on December 12, 1531, an Indian named Juan Diego had a vision of the Virgin Mary, the mother of Jesus. Some believers approach the shrine on their knees. Others sing and dance on the plaza in front of the monument. Boys dress up as Juan Diego, wearing traditional clothes and painting mustaches on their young faces. Other people dress in Indian costumes. Those who cannot travel to Mexico City celebrate the day with a fiesta in their own hometown.

The Games **People Play**

(Left) **Soccer players compete on a field near a cemetery.** (Right) **A banderillero, whose job is to weaken the bull in a bullfight, waves a red cape in front of the animal to make it run.**

Soccer is one of the most popular sports in Mexico. In Spanish, it's called *fútbol*. Adults and children play fútbol. They choose sides and set up goals in the streets and on playgrounds and soccer fields.

Mexicans also enjoy baseball, which they call *beisbol*. Some Mexican beisbol players join professional teams in the United States. Fernando Valenzuela is a very popular baseball player from Mexico. Players from the United States have also headed south to play in the Mexican league.

The Spanish brought bullfighting to Mexico. Many Mexican towns have a bullring. Bullfights take place on Sunday afternoons. Mexico City has the largest bullring in the world. It is called the Plaza de México. There are seats for 50,000 spectators. You can buy a seat in the shade or a seat in the sun. Seats in the sun cost less.

dor can study its charge. Next, the picador rides a horse in the ring and uses a lance to weaken the bull's neck muscles. The banderillero then jabs the bull with three pair of darts. The picadors and banderilleros are supposed to make the matador's job easier.

The matador's job is to kill the bull with a sword. He must work quickly but carefully. The horns of the bull are long and sharp, and the bull is quite strong. Matadors have about a one-in-ten chance of being killed in the bullring.

There are three different kinds of bullfighters—banderilleros, picadors, and matadors. A banderillero begins by using a cape to entice the bull about the ring, so that the mata-

¡Al Bate!*

*That's "Batter Up!" in Spanish

Many Mexicans are baseball fans, rooting for teams such as the Diablos Rojos (Red Devils) of Mexico City and the Jalisco state Guerreros (Warriors). Sometimes players from Mexican teams join the U.S. major leagues. Fernando Valenzuela, whom Mexicans call "El Toro" (the Bull), is a famous pitcher from Sonora. He won the Rookie of the Year and Cy Young Awards while playing for the Los Angeles Dodgers but has been with the San Diego Padres since 1995. Other Mexican-born players are New York Mets pitcher Armando Reynoso from San Luis Potosí, and Colorado Rockies infielder Vinny Castilla from Oaxaca.

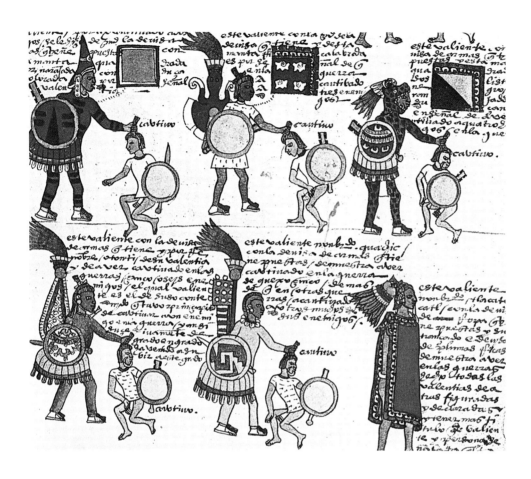

Not many Aztec writings survived the Spaniards' takeover of Mexico in the 1500s. This page is from the *Codex Mendoza,* a Spanish document that was based on an earlier Aztec book. The codex lists goods, crops, minerals, and other items available in Aztec lands.

Story **Time**

Mexico is a land of storytellers. Long ago Mayan priests recorded events in books made out of tree bark. They used an alphabet of pictures and symbols that stood for words and ideas. The Aztecs also used **pictographs** to tell the stories of their past.

In 1539 the first printing press in the **Western Hemisphere** began producing books in Mexico City.

Mexican newsstands and bookstalls offer all kinds of publications, from the comic-book stories of the caped crusader Super Barrio to more serious works by some of Mexico's great writers and poets.

Since then Mexico has made more books than any other country in **Latin America.** Small novels with drawings that illustrate the action are very popular in Mexico. So are *Foto-novelas*, which tell a story only with photographs.

An Aztec Tale

This tale explains how the Aztecs came to be.

A long time ago, all human beings were killed in a flood. Later the god Quetzalcoatl tricked the god of the underworld into giving up the bones of the dead. Quetzalcoatl ground the bones into a fine powder and mixed them with his own blood to create the Aztecs. Some of the bones were large, and some were small. That's why men and women come in different shapes and sizes.

José Clemente Orozco painted this mural in Guadalajara. It depicts the Mexican priest Miguel Hidalgo y Costilla, who led Mexico's drive for independence. In 1810 Hidalgo called on his fellow citizens to rebel against Spanish rule.

The Big **Picture**

Another way of telling a story is through paintings. Murals are huge paintings on walls or ceilings.

Mayan and Toltec painters were Mexico's original muralists. Hundreds of years later three famous painters created many important murals in Mexico. José Clemente Orozco, David Alfaro Siqueiros, and Diego Rivera painted many works on the walls of public buildings. Some of these murals show important scenes from Mexico's history.

Looking at Rivera's murals, for example, people can learn about the clash of the conquistadores (conquerors, or Spanish soldiers) with the

Aztec king, Montezuma. In another Rivera mural, peasant farmers struggle to scratch a living from land they don't own. In still another, the Mexican army fights U.S. forces along the Rio Grande. Just think—instead of reading about Mexican history, you can study it by looking at murals!

Mexican murals can teach a lot about the past. The country's most famous mural is perhaps *The History of Mexico* that Diego Rivera painted in Mexico City's National Palace.

Frida Kahlo

Have you ever made a picture of something that bothered or hurt you? The Mexican painter Frida Kahlo (1907–1954) did just that. In 1925 she was badly injured in a bus accident that left her partly crippled. To help her deal with the pain, Kahlo began to paint, mostly images of herself. These self-portraits show her both sick and healing, lonely and content.

After participating in a *charreada,* or rodeo, male and female riders often perform traditional dances in their riding costumes.

Music and **Dance**

Because the weather in Mexico is warm year-round, Mexicans spend much of their time outside. They walk on the streets and in the plazas. Music—coming from cars, from radios in shops, and from musicians who perform on the sidewalks—can be heard everywhere.

In some towns, a concert takes place on Sunday nights in the plaza.

A mariachi band plays while people walk by or watch from a café. Most mariachi bands have guitars, trumpets, violins, and a singer. They play Mexican folk music. The members dress in *charro* clothing, the traditional cowboy outfit.

During a fiesta, dancers perform in costume. Women may wear *chinas poblanas,* the traditional dresses of Mexico.

Flying Dancers

The Totonac Indians, who live near the port of Veracruz, still practice an ancient ceremony called the Voladores. The Volodores involves four men who have ropes wound around their waists. The ends of the ropes are tied to the top of a high pole or tower. The four men jump head first from the tower. The tower spins around 13 times, the ropes unwind, and the men dance and twist their way to the ground. At the last minute, they turn rightside-up and land on their feet. The Voladores is an amazing sight!

To the ancient Totonacs, the ceremony symbolized the calendar and the seasons. The Voladores ceremony is performed for thousands of tourists every year. The deeper meaning of the ritual has almost been forgotten.

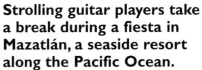

Strolling guitar players take a break during a fiesta in Mazatlán, a seaside resort along the Pacific Ocean.

41

Arts and **Crafts**

Mexican artwork and crafts are famous throughout the world. Artists in Mexico are proud to make things by hand. They often use age-old methods passed on from generation to generation to construct their crafts. These wares are sold on the streets, in the plazas, and at the marketplace.

Mexican pottery comes in hundreds of styles. Some potters shape their pieces by hand and then glaze (or coat) them with a thin layer of shiny paint. Animals, trees, and other natural designs are then painted on the surface of the pottery. Next the potters place their handiwork in hot kilns (ovens) or over open fires to harden the glaze.

Weavers create clothing, hammocks, rugs, mats, and many other goods. Many markets sell huipiles (embroidered cotton shirts), serapes (blankets), rebozos (shawls), and sombreros (hats).

These Indian craftworkers in Oaxaca weave blankets and other goods by hand.

Jewelers make their wares from Mexican copper, gold, or silver. Taxco, west of Mexico City, is a big silver town. Vendors there set up large wooden boards that hold hundreds of bright silver earrings, rings, necklaces, and bracelets.

Wood-carvers make painted masks and household objects such as chocolate stirrers. In the southern city of Puebla, small factories make brightly painted Talavera tiles that decorate the outside of many buildings. This craft was brought to Mexico from Spain.

Craftworks

Feeling creative? *Papel picado* is a brightly colored paper with fancy cutout designs. Several of the papers are strung together as decorations for fiestas in Mexico. Making a papel picado is fun. All you need is paper and a pair of scissors.

Here's what you do:
1. Take a sheet of colorful tissue paper (30 x 20 inches is a good size) and cut it in quarters to make four equally sized pieces. Each piece will measure 15 x 10 inches.
2. Fold one of the pieces in half the short way. Fold the paper in half twice more.
3. Cut away sections from the folded edges to form a design. Be careful not to cut all the way from one edge to another. The paper will fall apart!

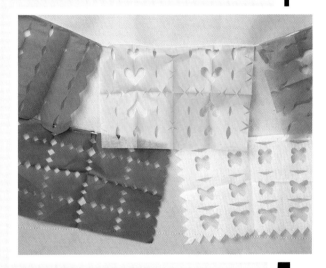

4. Repeat the above steps to the other three pieces. Unfold the papers. Glue or staple one edge of each papel picado to a long piece of string so they hang in a row. Papel picado banners make great decorations for parties or fiestas.

A Mayan statue from Chichén Itzá

Glossary

basin: A bowl-shaped region, often surrounded by highlands or mountains.

colony: A territory ruled by a country that is located far away.

the Conquest: Spain's forcible takeover of Mexico that began in the early 1500s. Because of this event, Mexicans speak Spanish and follow some Spanish customs.

desert: A dry, sandy region that receives low amounts of rainfall.

ethnic group: A large community of people that shares a number of social features in common, such as language, religion, or customs.

hemisphere: One half of the earth's surface. A globe, when divided vertically, shows the **Western Hemisphere** and the Eastern Hemisphere.

hurricane: A very strong windstorm that begins over the ocean, picks up large amounts of rain, and can cause severe damage when striking land.

immigrant: A person who moves from the home country to another country.

Latin America: The parts of the Western Hemisphere that were settled by Spaniards and that in modern times are governed by their descendants.

marsh: An area of soft, wet, low-lying land that is sometimes partly or wholly under water.

megalopolis: A very large city.

missionary: A person sent out by a religious group to spread its beliefs to other people.

peninsula: A piece of land that has water on three of its sides. The fourth side is connected to land.

orphan: A child without living parents.

pictograph: A picture used in a system of writing.

plateau: A region of level land that is above most of the surrounding territory.

shantytown: A poor neighborhood with makeshift housing and no indoor plumbing.

tropical rain forest: A dense, green forest that receives large amounts of rain every year. These forests lie at the equator.

volcano: An opening in the earth's surface through which hot, melted rock and gases are thrown up with explosive force. Volcano can also refer to the hill or mountain of ash and rock that builds up around the opening.

Girls strolling after school in the mercado

Pronunciation Guide

Baja	BAH-hah
Barranca del Cobre	bahr-RAHN-kah dehl KOH-bray
Belize	beh-LEEZ
Benito Juarez	bay-NEE-toh WAH-rehs
bienvenidos	bee-ehn-veh-NEE-dohs
Chichén Itzá	chee-CHEHN eet-ZAH
Chihuahua	chee-WAH-wah
chinas poblanas	CHEE-nahs poh-BLAH-nahs
La Conquista	lah kohn-KEES-tah
criollo	kree-OY-yoh
David Alfaro Siqueiros	dah-VEED ahl-FAHR-oh see-KAY-rohs
Día de los Muertos	DEE-ah day lohs MWEHR-tohs
Guadalajara	gwah-dah-lah-HAH-rah
Guadalupe	gwah-dah-LOO-pay
huipile	wee-PEE-lay
indígena	ihn-DEE-hay-nah
Iztaccíhuatl	ees-tahk-SEE-wahtl
jalapeño	hah-luh-PAY-nyoh
José Clemente Orozco	hoh-SAY klay-MAYN-tay oh-ROHS-koh
José Guadalupe Posada	hoh-SAY gwah-dah-LOO-pay poh-SAH-dah
Juan Diego	WAHN dee-AY-goh
México	MAY-hee-koh
Nueva España	NWAY-vah ehs-PAH-nyah
Oaxaca	wah-HAH-kah
Popocatépetl	poh-poh-kah-TAY-pehtl
quinceañera	keen-say-ah-NYEH-rah
serape	seh-RAH-pay
Sierra Madre	see-EHR-rah MAH-dray
Tenochtitlán	tay-nohk-teet-LAHN
Teotihuacán	tay-oh-tee-wah-KAHN
Voladores	voh-lah-DOH-rehs

Further Reading

Bierhorst, John, ed. *The Monkey's Haircut and other Stories Told by the Maya*. New York: William Morrow & Company, 1986.

Coronado, Rosa. *Cooking the Mexican Way*. Minneapolis: Lerner Publications Company, 1982.

DeVarona, Frank. *Benito Juarez: President of Mexico*. Brookfield, CT: Millbrook Press, 1993.

Goldstein, Ernest. *The Journey of Diego Rivera*. Minneapolis: Lerner Publications Company, 1995.

Mexico in Pictures. Minneapolis: Lerner Publications Company, 1994.

Silverthorne, Elizabeth. *Fiesta!: Mexico's Great Celebrations*. Brookfield, CT: The Millbrook Press, 1992.

Staub, Frank. *Children of the Sierra Madre*. Minneapolis: Carolrhoda Books, Inc., 1996.

Staub, Frank. *Children of the Yucatan*. Minneapolis: Carolrhoda Books, Inc., 1996.

Stein, R. Conrad. *The Aztec Empire*. New York: Marshall Cavendish, 1996.

Stein, R. Conrad. *Mexico City*. New York: Children's Press, 1996.

Tabor, Nancy M. *El Gusto Del Mercado Mexicano: A Taste of the Mexican Market*. Watertown, MA: Charlesbridge Publishing, Inc., 1996.

Temko, Florence. *Traditional Crafts from Mexico and Central America*. Minneapolis: Lerner Publications Company, 1996.

Wolf, Bernard. *Beneath the Stone: A Mexican Zapotec Tale*. New York: Orchard Books, 1994.

Metric Conversion Chart

WHEN YOU KNOW:	MULTIPLY BY:	TO FIND:
teaspoon	5.0	milliliters
Tablespoon	15.0	milliliters
cup	0.24	liters
inches	2.54	centimeters
feet	0.3048	meters
miles	1.609	kilometers
square miles	2.59	square kilometers
degrees Fahrenheit	5/9 (after subtracting 32)	degrees Celsius

Index